FINANCIAL**HOPE**

FINANCIAL
HOPE

Find Freedom in Your Finances
Through God's Word

MICHAEL BLUE

RON BLUE
INSTITUTE
For Financial Planning

The Ron Blue Institute for Financial Planning exists to equip people to understand biblical principles of finance so that they can live lives fully devoted to following Jesus.

First Printing: 2019
ISBN 978-1-9998673-1-0

Ron Blue Institute for Financial Planning, LLC
4201 S. Washington St.
Marion, Indiana 46953
www.ronblueinstitute.com

Contents

Introduction

The Bible has more to say about money than any other single topic. There are over 2,000 verses in the Bible about money and possessions, and 16 of Jesus' 38 parables deal with money. Simply put, the Bible talks a lot about money. With so much said in the Bible about money, you'd expect churches to talk about it regularly. But they don't. Why is that?

Money is one of the most private topics in our society and is rarely discussed. It can be surrounded by issues of shame, guilt, or control—no matter how much or little a person has. I believe that churches don't talk about money very often for fear of being perceived as self-serving. This shouldn't be the case. Our view of money impacts our view of God. Not only that, but our relationship with money impacts our relationship with God. Jesus tells us, "No one can serve two masters, for either he will hate the one and love the other, or he will be devoted to the one and despise the other. You cannot serve God and money" (Matthew 6:24). Jesus makes it clear that it isn't just difficult to serve God and money, it's impossible. We must make a choice. Either serve God or serve money. There is no other way.

Because of this choice we all must make, it behooves us to know what the Bible says about money (and it says a lot). If we don't know what the Bible says about money and how it affects our relationship with God, then we will tend to take the path of least resistance and follow the example of our culture. In my experience, this path rarely leads to contentment and freedom, and it almost always leads to serving money instead of God.

The Bible's teachings on money and possessions lead to contentment, freedom, and peace. The reason there is such a different result when we follow the Bible's teachings on money is that the Bible contains timeless and transcendent wisdom. The Bible's wisdom is true no matter when it is applied, and it is true no matter who is applying it. Simply put, it is always right, always relevant, and will never change. These truths have been proven over more than 3,000 years, and remain as applicable to us today as they were to Abraham in the ancient world.

The wisdom from the Bible about money represents the "why" behind our actions and not simply the "what and how." When applying biblical wisdom, we can be confident that our decisions are based on eternal truth and encompass both the "why and the how." This is why we explore the principles of biblical wisdom on money and possessions in this study. They can be applied to anybody in any situation and still be true. They can help us address the biggest questions in our lives. And they give us confidence in the decisions we make and peace no matter the outcome.

This study will explore what the Bible says about money and possessions and how that might impact your day to day life and your eternal purpose. Before you begin with this study, take a moment to assess how you feel about how are you doing with managing your money right now by completing the personal assessment below.

This assessment is designed to help you to be able to apply the biblical wisdom we will study over the next eight sessions to your current situation. There are no right or wrong answers here, just answer the questions based on where you are in relationship to your money today.

HEART:

Assess how your heart aligns with the four beliefs listed.

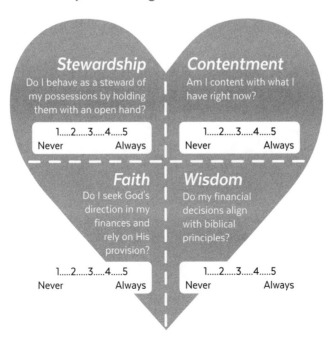

Stewardship
Do I behave as a steward of my possessions by holding them with an open hand?

1.....2.....3.....4.....5
Never   Always

Contentment
Am I content with what I have right now?

1.....2.....3.....4.....5
Never   Always

Faith
Do I seek God's direction in my finances and rely on His provision?

1.....2.....3.....4.....5
Never   Always

Wisdom
Do my financial decisions align with biblical principles?

1.....2.....3.....4.....5
Never   Always

HABITS:

Assess your strengths and weaknesses in the five essential biblical money management habits:

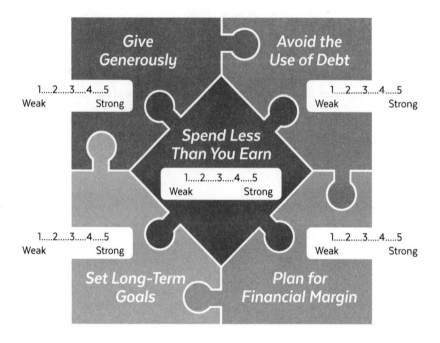

HEALTH:

Complete the pie below to identify your current reality of how you are spending your money:

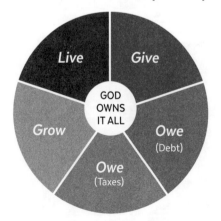

To calculate the percentages for your pie, record the following amounts and divide each by your income:

INCOME: $_____ %
GIVE: $_____ %
OWE (Debt): $_____ %
OWE (Taxes): $_____ %
GROW (Save): $_____ %
LIVE*: $_____ %

*LIVE = Income – (Give + Owe Debt + Owe Taxes + Grow)

HOPE:

Place an 'X' where you are and a '✓' where you want to be on the Margin Meter below.

Now that you know where you are, let's spend the next eight sessions developing a framework to help you make any needed changes to your current situation and a perspective to help you make future decisions about money. At the end of this study, you will have another opportunity to complete this assessment. We pray that you will feel more confident and content in your finances and be prepared to live fully into the life God has called you to live.

Money is a terrible master, but it is a terrific servant. Let's explore what the Bible says about our money and possessions, and then let's move together toward using the money God has blessed us with to make His name and glory known in all the world!

1

God Owns It All

PSALM 24:1

*The earth is the Lord's, and everything in it, the world,
and all who live in it.*

Have you ever considered the implications of Psalm 24:1? If everything in the world, including us, is God's, how does that affect how we live? John Wesley is a man who took this truth to heart in how he lived.

Born in 1703, the 15th of 19 children, John Wesley is best known as one of the founders of the Methodist church. He was so intent on getting the word of God into the hands of as many people as possible that he wrote short booklets and sold them for pennies. The demand for these booklets was remarkable and John Wesley became wealthy. Despite his significant wealth, Wesley never increased his lifestyle. In fact, he gave away any excess money he ever had. Not only was

Wesley generous with his money, he was also generous with his time. He is said to have ridden more than 250,000 miles and preached more than 40,000 sermons. He died at the age of 88 surrounded by friends and having given away nearly all his money. He believed that all he had was God's and lived this way with abandon. John Wesley had much and he gave much. He lived a life fully devoted to God.

The way we live our lives reflects our beliefs about God. Wesley's life reflected His belief in God's goodness and generosity. When we say we believe something, but our lives do not reflect that belief, then we are living inconsistently. Most Christians wouldn't hesitate to say that God owns everything. However, most of us live drastically differently from that belief.

Until our lives reflect our belief that God is the owner and provider of all things (money, time, intellect, relationships, etc.), our hearts will be closed off to the powerful work that God can do through our money. The world wants us to believe that our things are ours and we can do with them whatever we want. This mentality is the opposite of God's revealed reality.

When we live consistently with our belief that God owns it all, we begin seeing ourselves as stewards and not owners. We go from exercising the final say over our things to seeking God's will in all things. How we respond to God's ownership affects our relationship with Him. If we do not align our lives with this reality, then we will always feel like we are fighting against God for control of our things. When our lives reflect the belief of God's ownership, we become free to live lives like John Wesley's as we seek to glorify God in all things.

EXPLORING PSALM 24:1

Who owns the earth and all who live on it?

What does this reality imply about God, about you, and about your circumstances?

"The earth is the Lord's"

Read JOB 38:1-11. What things has God done and known that we cannot grasp?

How does God's overwhelming knowledge give you confidence to live the life that He has given you?

How does God's infinite understanding of creation shape your view about the ownership of your life and your things?

"And everything in it"

According to PSALM 50:9-12, does God lack anything? Why is that significant?

If everything is already God's, what is the significance of offering anything (our lives, our money, etc.) back to Him?

Read DEUTERONOMY 8:10-18. What is the danger of failing to acknowledge God as the provider and owner of all that you have?

Verse 10 tells us to bless the Lord for the things He has given us. How does a spirit of gratitude help reinforce your belief that God is the provider of everything?

How might having a spirit of entitlement and ownership affect your relationship with God?

"The world, and all who live in it"

Read MATTHEW 25:14-30. Who gave the slaves their talents and to whom were the slaves required to repay those talents?

Is there a greater or lesser burden you feel when you are caring for someone else's possessions instead of your own? Why do you feel that way?

Do you experience fear or excitement when you consider that God has entrusted His resources to you?

APPLYING PSALM 24:1

How can your behavior provide evidence that you believe God owns everything? List one or two practical ways you can work out this belief.

Take a few moments to thank God for all He has given you, specifically noting a few of the material blessings you enjoy.

2

Content with What I Have

HEBREWS 13:5

Keep your life free from love of money,
and be content with what you have, for He has said,
"I will never leave you nor forsake you."

Despite the nearly universal understanding that money doesn't buy happiness, most people still pursue money as a solution to their problems, worries, and fears. Why do we live as if we believe that more money leads to more happiness, when we know it won't?

At the beginning of their ministry, Bill and Vonette Bright, the founders of Cru (formerly known as Campus Crusade for Christ), wrote a contract committing all they had and everything they would make to God. This meant that they would have to rely on God for their needs and trust Him absolutely in everything that they did. Despite never having significant wealth, the Bright's lives were filled with adventure and influence. They lived in complete surrender and reliance on God, and God used them in ways that defy explanation.

In 1996, Bill's commitment was tested when he was awarded $1,000,000 as part of the prestigious Templeton Prize. He immediately gave the money away. When he was later asked if it had been hard to give away that much money, he responded that it wasn't, because he had given it away decades earlier in his contract with God. Knowing that contentment could only be found in God and that they would always be susceptible to the allure of wealth, the Brights ordered their lives to prioritize dependence on God over attaining wealth. As a result, their story is a testimony of God's tremendous blessing and faithfulness.

Even after we hear stories like these, it is still tempting to believe that more money is the solution to something in our lives. Money certainly is useful and necessary. However, the danger comes when we begin believing that money is our savior and the solution to our struggles. This mindset moves us to a love of money—meaning that money, instead of God, becomes our answer.

Until we can say like Paul, "in any circumstance I have learned the secret of being content," and we have acknowledged that the amount we have has nothing to do with that contentment, we will struggle with a love of money. Money is not evil, but it is dangerous. The Brights recognized this, ordered their lives to safeguard themselves, and never looked back. If we do not learn to be content with what we have right now, we will not be content when our resources grow.

EXPLORING HEBREWS 13:5

What does a life that loves money look like?

What truth about God does the writer of Hebrews tie to contentment? How might this truth speak to your own struggle with contentment?

"Keep your life free from love of money"

Read 1 TIMOTHY 6:6-10. What does Paul need to be content?

Why does Paul warn against a desire to be rich?

Does Paul say it is wrong to be rich?

What does loving money lead people to?

"Be content with what you have"

Are you content with what you have right now?

Read PHILIPPIANS 4:11-13. What is Paul's "secret" to contentment?

How have you experienced learning contentment as a process in your life?

Read JAMES 1:17. How does the reality that everything you have and everything you are is a gift from God impact you?

How can gratitude lead you toward contentment?

"I will never leave you nor forsake you"

Take a minute to write a short list of the most important material things, relationships, and immaterial things in your life.

Read MATTHEW 6:25-33. How does God's care for birds and lilies provide assurance that what you have today is enough?

When you find that you are anxious about financial things, where do you usually turn? How might this passage change your perspective on financial worries?

APPLYING HEBREWS 13:5

How can you more boldly rely on God as your provider and source of confidence, fostering greater contentment in the coming days and weeks?

Take a few moments to ask God to give you discernment about where in your life a love of money could be taking root.

3

Pursuing Faith in My Finances

HEBREWS 11:6

And without faith it is impossible to please Him,
for whoever would draw near to God must believe that
He exists and that He rewards those who seek Him.

Faith bridges our current reality and future hopes. It is the key to drawing closer to God and becoming the person He has made us to be. To live by faith requires trusting someone else. And trust is something many of us don't want to give away.

Dan had a hard time with trust. He worked in full-time ministry and longed to live by faith. His job required him to raise support, and he believed that God did not want him asking for money. This seeming contradiction provided ample opportunity for Dan to learn trust.

One year, a week before Christmas, Dan was out of money. When he told his wife that there would be no Christmas presents for their three young boys, she was heartbroken. Devastated, Dan marched to his office and began composing letters asking for money. If God wasn't going to come through, then Dan wasn't going to let his family down. In this moment, Dan felt the conviction of the Holy Spirit asking him if he wanted to do life his way or God's way. All he needed was a little faith.

God was giving Dan an opportunity to learn faith and trust. What would you have done?

Dan tore up his newly written letters and waited. That month Dan and his family saw God provide more financial support than they had ever received. Dan did not know what would happen when he tore up his letters, but he knew in whom he was placing his trust.

Exercising faith is never easy. If it was, it wouldn't be called faith. Faith stretches us and molds us into people who trust God implicitly. Without faith, we cannot please God. Without trust, we cannot have faith.

Faith in our finances means seeking God's direction, and then ordering our spending, saving, and giving in accordance with the convictions God has given us. Seeking God's direction in our finances is a tangible way to draw near to God and to live in a way that evidences a belief that He is the owner of everything that we possess and a trust that He cares for us no matter what.

EXPLORING HEBREWS 11:6

According to this verse, having faith means believing two specific things. What are those two things?

How does God being a rewarder of those who seek Him encourage you to exercise your faith in Him?

"Without faith it is impossible to please Him"

According to HEBREWS 11:1, what is the definition of faith?

How would having a confident faith like this affect your own walk with God?

Read *HEBREWS 11:23-28.* What did Moses choose to endure or give up on the basis of his faith?

Read *ROMANS 14:22-23.* According to these verses, how does having faith in daily actions free you before God? Conversely, how does doubting God's direction and provision in daily actions condemn you?

Are there any financial patterns or habits that you persist in doing, even while believing that you shouldn't do them?

"Whoever would draw near to God must believe that He exists"

What difference does believing that God exists make in a person's life?

How does the way you currently handle your money evidence your belief that God exists? What changes do you want to implement to make this more of a reality?

Romans 14:5 tells you to be fully convinced in your own mind when you take a stand of faith. Why is it so important for you to be fully convinced in your own mind that God exists?

Read **JAMES 2:18-19.** *Is simple mental assent/belief in the existence of God the type of belief God desires from you? Why or why not?*

"He rewards those who seek Him"

Read MATTHEW 25:24-30. What did fear cause the servant who received the one talent to do or not do?

How did the servant's fear of the master impact his ability to trust his master's intentions?

Has fear of God's character or fear of the future ever kept you from acting in faith? If so, how?

According to MATTHEW 6:31-33, what is the reward for seeking God?

How can you seek God in your finances?

APPLYING HEBREWS 11:6

Write down a significant financial decision you have been contemplating recently. Ask God what He would have you do in that situation. Begin to make it a habit to ask God what He would have you to do in your financial life.

4

Aligning Your Heart with God's

MATTHEW 6:20-21

*But lay up for yourselves treasures in heaven,
where neither moth nor rust destroys and where
thieves do not break in and steal. For where your
treasure is, there your heart will be also.*

John 3:16 is probably the most familiar Bible verse today. "For God so loved the world, that he gave his only Son." Did you catch that? Did you catch what God's love compelled Him to do?

Give. It's that simple. Giving is the ultimate expression of love.

Catherine worked an hourly job at a bakery and saw it as a part of her job to pray for her customers. She dreamed of one day owning a car and had managed to save $5,000 for that purpose. Through her church, she became aware of a woman in need and wanted to help. After much thought and prayer, she felt led to give this woman all her car savings. Questioning whether she had done the right thing, she sheepishly shared this story with a regular customer. The customer was so moved by Catherine's generosity that she and her husband decided to buy Catherine a brand-new car. Catherine was blown away by their generosity. When asked about why she gave away her hard-earned savings, she said, "We don't give in order to receive. We give because it's the nature of Jesus Christ. He gave us His life, so we have the DNA of Jesus Christ, [the DNA] of giving."[1]

Catherine did not give to receive; she gave because she loved. If we want to act like our Heavenly Father and express our love for Him and other people, we give. The very nature of God is to love. The natural expression of that love is giving. And when we give, our hearts become aligned with God's character.

Not only is giving the way to align our hearts with God's, it is also the thing that will bring us the most joy for all of eternity. Giving demonstrates love, expresses the Gospel, moves our heart toward God, and brings us joy. If all these things are true, then we would be foolish not to pursue the riches of generosity! Aligning our hearts with God is the best thing we can do for today and eternity.

---

1   The video of this story can be seen at generousgiving.org/media/videos/i-like-car.

EXPLORING MATTHEW 6:20-21

How does putting your treasure in heaven move your heart toward heaven?

What do you think it means to lay up treasures in heaven?

"Lay up for yourselves treasures in heaven"

Read MATTHEW 25:31-46. What were those on the King's right hand doing to lay up treasures in heaven?

What do you think motivated these people on the King's right hand to provide food for the hungry, water for the thirsty, shelter the stranger, clothes for the naked, and company for the prisoner?

1. *According to Luke 6:38, what is the result of our giving?*

"Where neither moth nor rust destroys and where thieves do not break in and steal"

Read 2 CORINTHIANS 8:9. How do we become rich?

What does it mean to be rich in the way this verse describes?

According to LUKE 12:16-21, what happens to your plentiful produce when you die?

What is a plentiful produce that will last after you die?

"For where your treasure is, there your heart will be also"

According to LUKE 16:13, what two things does Jesus say we cannot serve at the same time?

Why do you think that the love of money leads to hating and despising God?

What are some practical things you can do to move your heart toward God and away from a love of money?

APPLYING MATTHEW 6:20-21

Does the way you use your money reflect where you want your treasure to be? If not, how could you begin to change the way you use your money so that it does?

Take a few moments to ask God to help you align how you use your money with His heart.

5

Using Money as a Tool

1 TIMOTHY 6:17

As for the rich in this present age, charge them
not to be haughty, nor to set their hopes on
the uncertainty of riches, but on God,
who richly provides us with everything to enjoy.

In 1959 John Steinbeck wrote, "We can stand anything God and nature can throw at us save only plenty. If I wanted to destroy a nation, I would give it too much and would have it on its knees, miserable, greedy and sick."[2] What an amazingly prophetic statement about American culture. Despite living in one of the wealthiest countries in the world, Americans can't seem to find enjoyment or contentment in their abundance of things. Why is this so?

---

2 John Steinbeck, letter to Adlai Stevenson, Guy Fawkes Day 1959, as quoted in *Letters of Note* (online, cited 28 April 2016). Available from the Internet: lettersofnote.com.

R.G. LeTourneau is credited with creating the modern mechanized earthmoving industry. His company built 70% of the earthmoving equipment used by the Allies in World War II. Needless to say, he was very rich. Despite his tremendous success, he remained grounded in the reason for his existence—to glorify God and spread the good news of Jesus Christ. He used nearly all his money in pursuit of this purpose.

Whenever LeTourneau spoke he would begin by saying, "Friends, I'm just a sinner saved by grace. Just a mechanic that the Lord has blessed." He believed that his business was God's and that the money he made was a tool for accomplishing God's purposes. Even when finances became tight, LeTourneau continued giving away most of what he made, saying, "The question is not how much of my money I give to God, but rather how much of God's money I keep for myself."

LeTourneau solved the paradox highlighted by John Steinbeck. By using money to glorify God and proclaim His name, he discovered the antidote to his greed. Money became nothing more than a tool for him to use for God.

When we believe that more money will satisfy our deepest longings, we pursue it, believing that happiness and success will closely follow. Money and things become the goal, and anything that prevents us from acquiring them becomes a hurdle to overcome. This is what Steinbeck saw.

But God intended money to be a tool, not a goal. Only when we view money as a tool to accomplish God-given goals and purposes does money move to its proper place in our lives, freeing us from the lie that more money is the answer to our fears and frustrations.

A life that puts its hope in money will never find freedom from fear and disappointment, while a life that puts its hope in God will find freedom and enjoyment in using money in the passionate pursuit of God's glory and the accomplishment of His purposes. When we embrace these truths, we begin to realize that every decision we make with money has spiritual implications (not just our giving decisions).

EXPLORING 1 TIMOTHY 6:17

Where are the rich told not to set their hope? Why?

Where are the rich told to set their hope? Why?

"As for the rich in this present age"

Read MATTHEW 19:16-26. Why do you think Jesus says that it is hard for a rich person to enter the kingdom of God?

What is it about riches that make it difficult for us to trust God?

Does the amount of money you have today have anything to do with your eternal destination? Why or why not?

"Charge them not to be haughty, nor to set their hopes on the uncertainty of riches"

Read REVELATION 3:17-20. What happened to the perspective of the rich people when they believed they didn't need anything?

How are the riches that Jesus tells us to pursue from Him better than the riches of earth? What is different about them?

Read ECCLESIASTES 5:10-15. If you love money, will you ever be satisfied with the amount you have? According to these verses, why is that the case?

What happens to your riches when you die?

"But on God, who richly provides us with everything to enjoy"

According to ECCLESIASTES 5:19, how could you view your life and work in your current season as a gift from God?

How does your day-to-day life evidence an enjoyment of the things that God has given you? Are there ways you could use money more intentionally that would remind you of the gifts God has given you?

According to PSALM 118:20-24, what is the ultimate reason for a Christian to rejoice? How does this gift of God inspire rejoicing in your heart today?

APPLYING 1 TIMOTHY 6:17

*How does understanding that money is merely a tool help you
enjoy what you have and set your hope on God rather than on the
money itself?*

*Take a few moments to thank God for His provision and to ask Him to
give you joy in the things He provides.*

6

Debt Mortgages Your Future

PSALM 37:21

The wicked borrows but does not pay back,
but the righteous is generous and gives.

T he Bible doesn't call debt a sin, but it does warn us about its many unintended consequences.

When I was a young lawyer, we moved to Austin, Texas, and bought a home not far from downtown. We could barely afford the home, but reasonably expected my income to steadily increase over time. Even if it didn't, Austin was a great real estate market, so we believed we could always sell the home at any time and get our money out.

About three years after we bought our home, I became convicted that my job had become unsustainable for my family and faith. Around this same time, the real estate market in the United States crashed. We couldn't sell our house. To make matters worse, I couldn't quit my job because I couldn't replace enough of my income in another job to still afford our mortgage. I was trapped. I literally owned a home that prevented me from taking a different job or going where I felt God leading me to go.

For three more years, we were unable to change anything. Eventually, the market recovered, we were able to sell our house and were finally freed to follow where God was leading. I learned a very important lesson along the way—debt always obligates me to something in the future before I know what the future holds.

By using debt, we are pre-committing our future selves to pay for our current wants and needs. Not only that, we are restricting our ability to be generous both now and in the future. We have reduced the amount of money that will be available in the future to meet unanticipated needs. In essence, debt says that our needs and wants today are worth more than anything the future brings.

Our decision about going into debt today is about a lot more than whether we can afford the payment. The decision is about whether we can afford to limit our futures. Debt always has future consequences; the trouble is that we can't know what they will be.

EXPLORING PSALM 37:21

Why do you think the righteous in this verse are able to give generously?

What are the root causes of not being able to repay a debt?

"The wicked borrows but does not pay back"

Read PROVERBS 22:7. How does the lender-borrower relationship mirror a slave owner-slave relationship?

How does being in debt to another put you in bondage to them?

*According to **PROVERBS 22:26-27**, what happens if you cannot repay what you owe?*

*Read **JAMES 4:13-16**. What is wrong with boasting about what you will do tomorrow?*

How do you reconcile making plans and goals for the future with these verses?

"The righteous is generous and gives"

*Read **LUKE 12:24**. Why can you afford to be generous?*

How could debt prohibit you from experiencing God's hand of provision?

Read **2 CORINTHIANS 8:2-5.** *How did these people view giving?*

How is your attitude toward giving similar to or different from these people?

Why do you think the Psalmist in **PSALM 37:21** *contrasts the borrower and the giver the way that he does?*

How might debt decrease your ability to give today?

APPLYING PSALM 37:21

Do you have any debt today that is preventing you from being as generous as you want to be? How might you approach debt differently if you thought about it based on the impact more debt would have on your ability to give?

Take a few moments to ask God to help you understand and see the connection between debt and your ability to be generous.

7

How Much is Enough?

PROVERBS 6:6 & 8

*Go to the ant, O sluggard; consider her ways
and be wise. . . She prepares her bread in summer
and gathers her food in harvest.*

Financial maturity means giving up today's desires for tomorrow's benefit. Saving for the future is biblical, prudent, and wise. However, as is true in all things, excessive saving can be both foolish and harmful to your spiritual life.

Randy Alcorn, founder of Eternal Perspective Ministries and well-known author, has lived on minimum wage for most of his adult life. While circumstances that he was unable to change dictated his limited income, he developed a unique perspective regarding how much his family needs to live as a result of it. Even with a very limited income, Randy writes about his own struggle to determine how much money he should save for retirement. He writes, "Nanci and I decided a while back to take out some retirement funds and give them to God's kingdom. But we still have a significant amount left. Some day we may give more of it away, or none of it, or all of it. I don't know. But I do know we must ask God, because it belongs to him, not us."[3]

Randy lives inside the tension of trying to be responsible in saving for the future while not accumulating so much that he has no need to rely on God. There are no easy answers here. He says, "Many financial counselors would tell me I'm not laying up nearly enough for retirement. But when I read Scripture, I wonder if I'm laying up too much. I live in this tension and I suppose it will never be resolved."[4] The most important thing for Randy (and us) is to leave room for God.

When we accumulate with no purpose or end in mind, we will never know when we have accumulated enough. We must begin any savings plan by answering the questions, "How much is enough?" and "What am I saving toward?" Until we have determined our needs and how much we believe God wants us to save, we run the risk of trying to use our savings to replace God.

There is a fine line between saving and hoarding. One is responsible and the other can undermine our faith. Are we trying to accumulate enough so that we don't need to rely on God? If so, we need to make a change.

3 Randy Alcorn, *Money, Possessions, and Eternity,* (Carol Stream, IL ,Tyndale, 2003), page 334.
4 Ibid., page 335.

Answering the question of "how much is enough?" is the best way to make sure we are being responsible, while guarding against trying to replace God as our provider. Spend some time with God asking Him to help you identify how much He wants you to save toward certain life contingencies (i.e. college, retirement, etc.). Look at the ant and be wise.

EXPLORING PROVERBS 6:6 & 8
What does an ant do that is wise?

If you were emulating what the ant is doing, what would you do and how much would you gather?

"Go to the ant, O sluggard; consider her ways and be wise"

According to JAMES 1:5, God gives us wisdom when we ask for it. How do you currently seek wisdom when you are making a difficult decision?

Read JAMES 3:17. Compare the way James describes wisdom from God with earthly wisdom that you have seen?

Do you believe that God's wisdom is true and available to anyone who asks? Why or why not?

"She prepares her bread in summer"

Read LUKE 14:28-30. What do you think would be included in the builder's list of costs involved in building the tower?

How much extra money do you think the builder should set aside over and above the cost of the tower?

According to PROVERBS 21:20, how can you distinguish between a foolish person and a wise person?

*How can you practice wisdom in making plans for how much you
save for the future?*

"And gathers her food in harvest"

Read LUKE 12:16-21. What is the man's mistake in this parable?

*What should this man have done before deciding what to do with
his excess of crop?*

*Your earthly goods are like manure, if you pile them up they begin to
stink, but if you spread them out they produce a harvest. Similarly, you
should be careful about gathering up more money and possessions
than you need. Once you have determined what you need, enjoy the
process of spreading the excess out by giving it away.*

APPLYING PROVERBS 6:6 & 8

How can you determine where the line is for you between wisely saving for the future and hoarding?

Take a few moments to ask God to help you determine how He wants you to use your resources to glorify Him.

8

A Hope for Tomorrow

PROVERBS 21:5

*The plans of the diligent lead surely to abundance, but
everyone who is hasty comes only to poverty.*

In 1813, 25-year-old Adoniram Judson and his new wife left their
families in America to become missionaries in Burma. Burma was
a place of incredible hostility with no missionary presence. Judson and
his wife spent six years living and working in Burma before they saw
their first convert to Christ. Afterwards, Judson's wife wrote to her
father, "Papa, after nearly six years in Burma we have a convert—and
that makes it all worthwhile!"[5] Six years of sacrifice for one soul and
she was ecstatic—what a great testimony of diligence and patience.

---

5 Irene Howat, *Adoniram Judson, Danger on the Streets of Gold,* (Scotland, Christian
  Focus Publishing, 2008), page 35.

For 38 years, Judson diligently sowed seeds of the Gospel without seeing major results. Today, however, there are over 3,700 congregations of Baptists and 1.9 million Christians in Burma that can trace their origins directly to Judson. Judson understood that the only way to grow the church in Burma was to diligently and patiently empty his life into the people. He didn't live to see the conversion of those millions of people, but he trusted God's purpose for his life.

Judson approached his calling with a long-term perspective. He understood that his primary role was to scatter seed diligently every day and then trust that God would produce an abundance in due time. Judson's life demonstrated that his hope was in eternity and the reward he sought was not to be found in this life. Because of his perspective, Judson jealously guarded his plans and always made sure that he left margin in his life so that he could easily respond to God's direction and leading. Without a plan and room for God to direct, he would not have lasted as long as he did in Burma. These same principles apply to us in our financial lives. If we don't diligently plan and provide room (i.e. margin) in our finances for God to work, we end up thrashing around frustrated by a sense that we are being controlled by our money rather than knowing that our financial life is being directed by God.

Financial margin rarely occurs unintentionally. It must be diligently planned for and protected. Without margin, our plans don't get realized and our hopes get dulled. We end up financially, emotionally, and mentally impoverished as living paycheck to paycheck taxes our ability to see beyond tomorrow.

When we get to this point, putting our hope in eternity becomes challenging since today's troubles loom so large. We will usually end up frustrated until that margin is found. Understood this way, margin serves as a barometer of our ability to focus our hope in eternity. If we want to experience the abundance that God has for us both now and in eternity, we must be diligent and patient as we jealously guard our margin. If we have no margin now, then we must change our habits to create it. Until we do this, our hearts will struggle to turn toward the hope of tomorrow.

EXPLORING PROVERBS 21:5

What do you think the writer of this verse means by the word abundance (i.e. abundance of what)?

What are some ways you have acted diligently in your finances and what are some ways you have acted hastily?

"The plans of the diligent lead surely to abundance"

Read ROMANS 12:2. How does God's will differ from the pattern of the world?

Read PROVERBS 4:20-27. What benefits are there for those who listen closely to godly instruction?

On whose plans do you think the person described in these verses is focused—his own or God's?

*According to **EPHESIANS 2:10**, when were your good works established by God?*

What does this tell us about whose plans we should be diligently pursuing?

"Everyone who is hasty comes only to poverty"

*Read **HEBREWS 5:12-14**. What do these verses say about people who do not move from living on milk to living on solid food?*

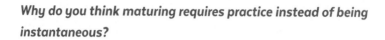

Why do you think maturing requires practice instead of being instantaneous?

*According to **ISAIAH 43:18-19**, how should you view your prior financial mistakes?*

If God can make a river in the desert, what can He help you do in your financial life?

*The only way to move toward the plans God has for you is to maintain margin in your budget and in your life. According to **PHILIPPIANS 3:14**, what should motivate you in pursuing margin in your financial life?*

What is God calling you to do today?

APPLYING PROVERBS 21:5

What plans do you need to make and apply diligently to be able to pursue the upward call of God in Christ Jesus?

What things can you change in your life today that will demonstrate to someone watching you that your hope is in eternity?

Post-Study Assessment

GALATIANS 2:20

*I have been crucified with Christ. It is no longer I
who live, but Christ who lives in me. And the life I now
live in the flesh I live by faith in the Son of God,
who loved me and gave himself for me.*

Abiblical approach to money management begins with understanding where you are in four main areas. Your Heart, Habits, Health, and Hope. The prior eight lessons have focused on each of these in detail. In order to make a plan for you to move to where you believe God is leading you, you need to first assess where you are today.

HEART:

Assess how your heart aligns with the four beliefs listed.

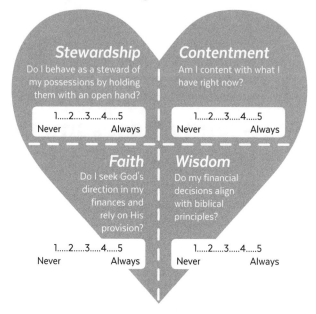

Stewardship
Do I behave as a steward of my possessions by holding them with an open hand?

1.....2.....3.....4.....5
Never   Always

Contentment
Am I content with what I have right now?

1.....2.....3.....4.....5
Never   Always

Faith
Do I seek God's direction in my finances and rely on His provision?

1.....2.....3.....4.....5
Never   Always

Wisdom
Do my financial decisions align with biblical principles?

1.....2.....3.....4.....5
Never   Always

HABITS:

Assess your strengths and weaknesses in the five essential biblical money management habits:

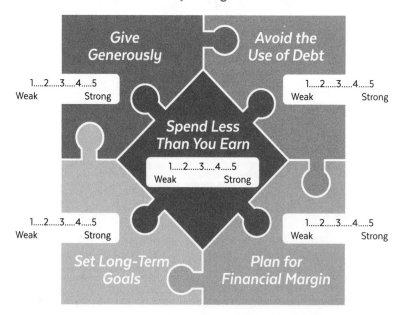

Give Generously

1.....2.....3.....4.....5
Weak   Strong

Avoid the Use of Debt

1.....2.....3.....4.....5
Weak   Strong

Spend Less Than You Earn

1.....2.....3.....4.....5
Weak   Strong

Set Long-Term Goals

1.....2.....3.....4.....5
Weak   Strong

Plan for Financial Margin

1.....2.....3.....4.....5
Weak   Strong

HEALTH:

**Complete the pie below to identify your current reality
of how you are spending your money:**

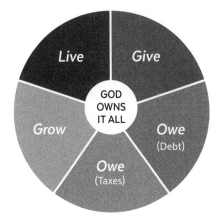

*To calculate the percentages for your
pie, record the following amounts
and divide each by your income:*

INCOME: $_____ %
GIVE: $_____ %
OWE (Debt): $_____ %
OWE (Taxes): $_____ %
GROW (Save): $_____ %
LIVE*: $_____ %

*LIVE = Income – (Give + Owe Debt + Owe Taxes + Grow)

HOPE:

**Place an 'X' where you are and a '✓' where you want to be
on the Margin Meter below.**

Based on your assessments above, what are your strengths in each of the four areas?

HEART:

HABITS:

HEALTH:

HOPE:

Based on your assessments above, what are your weaknesses in each of the four areas?

HEART:

HABITS:

HEALTH:

HOPE:

We always say that until you get your heart and beliefs fully submitted to God, it is difficult to make lasting changes in your finances. If you find that you are weak in one or more areas related to your heart, spend some time journaling why you think it is this way. Think about the way you watched your parents manage money, your first positive and negative experience with money, how you prefer to feel love, how your friends display their use of money, and how social media and advertising play a role in making you think about the sufficiency of what you have. Begin writing below and on the next page:

Once you begin to understand your heart, you should take account of your habits and assess your financial health. Are you practicing each of the five biblical habits for money management? Does your pie diagram reflect what you want your priorities to be? If you answered either of these questions in the negative, what changes do you need to make?

Finally, the only way to make progress toward your long-term goals is to increase your margin. This is where these concepts converge. You must change your habits to adjust your pie and increase your margin. This is the only way to make progress. What habits can you adopt to grow your margin to where you want to be?

How will you realign your pie based on your increase in margin?

Take a few moments to thank God for giving you everything you have and acknowledge Him as the owner of everything.

PROVIDING CHRISTIANS
ACCESS
TO BIBLICAL FINANCIAL WISDOM

Professionals | Colleges
High Schools | Churches | You

CHRISTIAN HIGH SCHOOL AND HOMESCHOOL PROGRAMS

COLLEGE CURRICULUM AND DEGREES

STEWARDSHIP COACH TRAINING

SMALL GROUP MATERIALS AND BOOKS

RON BLUE INSTITUTE